A Guide to Effective Solution for Reducing Prisonization

A Guide to Effective Solution for Reducing Prisonization

Omar Garrison

To order additional copies of this book, contact:
Xlibris Corporation
1-888-795-4274
www.Xlibris.com
Orders@Xlibris.com
97344

CONTENTS

Controlling the Effects of Prisonization

Corrections exist to punish criminals for crimes against society and to rehabilitate offenders to live a law-abiding life in the community. The penal system should be a main contributor assisting ex-offenders reintegration back into the community. Ample time is available for policy makers to reform policies that benefit inmates and employees. The central focus of penal reform actively continues with supporting corrections staff and inmates with proper resources. A suitable approach may be in making change an essential part of the penal system.

The adult prison population in 2005 was 1,446,269 (US Department of Justice, Bureau of Justice Statistics). This adult prison population is very different from 1980 when the prison population was 319,598. Unfortunately, those individuals in jail, on probation, and on parole increased the total adult population under the criminal justice system in 2005 to 7,056,000. The incarceration boom from 1980 up to the present day has forced many male and female inmates to relinquish personal freedom.

Purpose of the Guide

The purpose of this guide is to present scientific research information that may influence and provide criminal-justice policy makers evidence-based research in reforming corrections policies. Corrections leaders implement appropriate policy changes to enhance inmates' rehabilitation and employees' job satisfaction. This guide presents correctional leadership with information motivating subordinates to carry out structural changes.

Audience

This guide targets stakeholders, such as criminal justice policy makers, correctional personnel, families, and communities giving them an opportunity to suggest dramatic improvements in corrections. However, the primary responsibility to ensure workable correctional policies will take an assertive effort from research findings. Criminal-justice policy makers evaluating research findings can transform correctional policies. Correctional leaders can implement policy benefiting inmates and employees.

Background of the Problem

This practical guide may serve as a wake-up call to improve penitentiary conditions. Prisonization illustrates how some individuals bring deviant behavior into the prisons. This guide focuses particularly on prisonization as it logically links to inmate behavior uniquely to the prison environment. The guide demonstrates stages of how prisonization emerges in corrections. It also suggests steps corrections leaders can choose to transform prisonization.

The theoretical aspects of this guide demonstrate solutions to individual psychosocial development leading to societal maladjustment. The reference guide introduces organizational transformational strategies to reduce maladjustment in individuals. Additionally, the guide focuses on how responsible individuals may surrender personal freedom and still overcome prison adversities.

Leaders must ensure employees have proper training and knowledge in relation to transforming the penal system. Transforming the penal system may reduce prison violent and deviant actions. However, it is essential that researchers explain their findings in an understandable language.

Statement of the Problem

Prisonization is a slow-emerging problem that worsens the longer individuals stay in prison. The constant sequential exposure to violence handicaps individuals and also may contribute to maladjustment during their return to society.

How Prisonization Emerges

Inmates internalize prisonization through violent, abusive treatment in and exposure to the prison subculture. Inmate attitudes and time served in prison may determine whether they will embrace or reject the inmate code. Newly arrived individuals may become victims of rape, intimidation, and violence. In a prison environment, correctional staff enforces rules and regulations to control deviant behavior and rehabilitate inmates. Unfortunately, these same rules and regulations may be the very core of the prisonization problem. Of particular interest are the following:

1. After a year of confinement, most inmates surrender to the inmate code, rebel, and willingly engage in gang activities.
2. Inmates who served one to three years appear to split between submitting to inmate code, penal authority, and survival.
3. Lastly, inmates serving three years or more may relinquish their personal freedom and independence.

One other factor individuals relinquish is their identity as unique people. Overall prisonization happens mostly after inmates have spent a great deal of time confined (Grounds 2002; Jensen and Jones 2001; Turner 2006).

Table 1

Four Common Stages in Developing Prisonization

Period	Sequential Critical Event Exposure			
Stage 1 arrival	Rape	Intimidation	Sex slave	Violence
Stage 2 6 mo-1 yr	Inmate code	Rebellion	Gang activity	Violence
Stage 3 1-3 yrs	Acceptance of subculture	Submit to prison authority	Submit to inmate code	Violence
Stage 4 3+ yrs	Depend on inmate code for survival	Dependent on penal system for survival	Loss of independence	Violence

Note: Table 1 illustrates that longer sentences cause prisonization.

Consequence of Prisonization

Imprisonment is an environmental hazard that strips away inmates' freedom, comparable to a life-threatening hostage situation. Subsequently, the penal system gains control over the inmates' lives. The inmates gradually develop a dependency on the penal system for basic needs. Hostages go through a life-threatening process and eventually depend on their captors for basic needs. Comparatively, inmates and hostages share a motivation for survival. Underlying the definition of prisonization denotes incarceration as an agent of terror enhancing the Stockholm syndrome. The intensity and physical abuse from the perpetrator cause captives to develop signs of the Stockholm syndrome. Stockholm syndrome denotes captives thanking the perpetrator for sparing their lives as well as distrust and anger toward the authorities (Fabrique, Romano,

Vecchi, and Hasselt 2007; Thomas, Peterson, and Zingraff 1978; Zingraff 1975).

Behavioral Strategies

Researchers must distinguish the different coping mechanisms between four variables related to prison life: (a) overcoming adversity, (b) reestablishing control, (c) making an adjustment, and (e) making inmate choices. These variables should be clear and presentable to each criminal-justice policy makers. Well-defined variables enhance policy makers' interpretation of prisonization. Workable policies implemented by correctional staff assist inmates to overcome adversities (Fabrique et al. 2007; Jacobson 2006; Latessa 2004; Zingraff 1975).

Overcoming Adversities

Along with overcoming adversities are degrading treatment and restricted conditions. Fortunately, inmates who think positively and struggle to overcome stigmas associated with negative inmates' labeling, in comparison to those who think negatively and give in to the process. When inmates choose to accept the harsh prison conditions, protocol, and labeling, they can gradually transform and develop self-control (Buell 2005; DeLisi 2003; Hatcher 2006; Livers and Hoffman 2005; Stevens 1998; Winnick and Bodkin 2005).

Reestablishing Control

Importantly, inmates with self-control are aware of the odds against success in rebellious behavior. Inmates can take this wisdom a level further by willingly accepting the difficulties of penitentiary life. Self-motivation within the prison is another way to create routine rather than accept the prison's primary routine. Use each day to develop, adjust, and disregard the harsh conditions in prison (Frankl 2000; Johnson and Dobrzanska 2005; Lehrer 2001; Torres 2006).

Making an Adjustment

Prisonization eventually takes away an individual's capacity to make constructive choices. However, individuals can make good choices about their lifestyles while in prison. Inmates who have a sense of self-control will eventually adjust better. Individuals can intentionally choose to follow prison rules without behaving rebelliously or causing problems (Bandura 1998; Frankl 1984; Johnson and Dobrzanska 2005; Kenemore and Roldan 2006).

Making Inmate Choices

The pains of imprisonment on individuals have many different negative influences. Particularly affected are inmates who wander from place to place devoid of any constructive routine. They are hopelessly depressed and lack meaningful purpose in life. Unfortunately, these individuals fall prey to rape, abuse, violence, and dehumanization (Gillespie 2003; Jensen and Jones 2001; Johnson and Dobrzanska 2005).

Inmates who choose to avoid idling experience less violence. Inmates who unite with the community, politicians, and correctional officials can change some of the hopelessness experienced in prison. Male and female inmates' choices enhance their survival ratio and reduce prisonization (Haney 2001; Johnson and Dobrzanska 2005; Kerley, Matthews, and Blanchard 2005).

Effective long-range reform may come because correctional staff identifies inmates' specific needs. Female inmates are a minority of the total US imprisoned population and have needs essentially different from the majority male inmate population. Incarcerated female needs have been ignored, thus seriously evoking corrections to consider their well-being (Buell 2005; Craig 2006; Stevens 1998).

The penal systems that address females' needs will likely increase interest in their well-being. This is not to overlook male inmate needs. Lastly, inmates may undeniably benefit from having more responsibilities for their family, children, and a second chance at parenting (Buell 2005; Craig 2006; Jensen and Jones 2001; Travis 2006).

Family Participation

Humans are family oriented by nature. Thus, inmates needs include visits from (a) family, (b) children, and (c) friend. Importantly, when these needs are accommodated, the result may not lead to prisonization. Therefore, correctional staff can implement strategies benefiting inmates while helping employees understand inmate family needs (Stevens 1998; Torres 2006; Valle, Huang, and Spira 2006).

Family involvement is fundamental for incarcerated individuals. Family involvement enhances inmates' (a) efficiency, (b) self-esteem, and (c) self-efficacy. For example, Oregon Correctional facility provides female inmates interaction with family. This interaction among families provides inmates with self-efficacy essential to become law-abiding citizens. Interaction with family members also enhances positive attitudes with inmates at risk. Oregon Correctional facility intervention programs and services allow an opportunity at parenting through reuniting inmates with their children (Bandura 1998; Buell 2005; Chlup 2006; Craig 2006).

Importantly, families are the key to restoring inmate confidence for becoming successful upon release. Fortunately, Oregon Correctional family visits encourage other correctional institutions to implement positive family visitation programs. Researchers' findings speed up positive change through accurate investigation (Akbar 2004; Buell 2005; Chlup 2006; Jacobson 2006).

Use of Research Studies

Accurate research finding may serve in presenting (a) implementing policy reform, (b) communicating with stakeholders, (c) presenting findings in a nontechnical language, (d) presenting evidence-based results, and (e) conducting empirical investigation.

Determining positive reform may eventually come from researchers' findings. Regardless of the many facts researchers present to criminal-justice policy makers, the relevant evidence must be convincing enough to warrant policy reform. Researchers can "bridge the gap between theory, research, and practice" (Latessa 2004, 552) in an understandable language.

Furthermore, the understandable language presented illustrates relationship between independent and dependent variables. For example, a state that has decreased crime rates yet still has the fastest growing incarceration rates may need clarification by researchers. Clarifying research assists the criminal-justice policy makers' decision-making processes (Hatcher 2006; Jacobson 2006; Latessa 2004; Roberts and Hough 2005).

Policy Reform

Policy makers who receive research information concerning the rapid spread of infection (e.g., inmates who share personal items) can reform policy. Correctional leaders can implement the policy change. For example, inmates violate regulations by intentionally using other inmates' personal items. Violator punishment includes restrictive yard etc. Employee violations include giving and/or knowing inmates share personal items (Jacobson 2006; Lehrer 2001; Mall 2004; Turabelidze, Lin, Wolkoff, Dodson, Gladbach, and Zhu 2006).

Implementing Policy Change

Employees who presently work in the penal system often reject the idea of change. They are comfortable with the current policies and believe change will instantly bring complexity to their jobs (Latessa 2004; Livers and Hoffman 2005; Stevens *1998; Torres 2006; Winnick and Bodkin 2005).*

Correctional leaders may base implementing policy on people who have influences within the government. Correctional leaders acquire exception to labels indicating that they are soft on crime and oppose punishing criminals. Correctional leaders definitely hope to project a tough image on crime and show strong support for punitive measures. Simply not showing active aggressive measures against criminals may limit their fortunate position at implementing policy change (Alvin 2005; Jacobson 2006; Thomas et al 1978).

Incarcerated individuals have goals that give them purpose in life, such as (a) living with family, (b) gainful employment, and (c) furthering their education. Correctional leadership knows the pains of imprisonment that causes prisonization. They can become responsive and implement positive changes that will enhance employees understanding of inmates' daily experiences (Akbar 1995; Bandura 1998; Frankl 1984; Gillespie 2005; Kenemore and Roldan 2006; Travis 2006).

Leadership should implement the following safety measures:

1. Train guards to detect inmates who may be violent.
2. Monitor gang activities
3. Conduct cell searches for drugs and weapons
4. Advocate anti-inmates violence.

5. Encourage inmates to participate in programs changing the nature of their environment.

6. Introduce work programs.

7. Advocate educational programs

8. Conduct counseling sessions.

9. Encourage recreation participation.

10. Exemplify a family-friendly environment.

11. Introduce mechanisms to reduce prisonization.

Communicating with Stakeholders

Explaining research findings in nontechnical terms allow stakeholders to interpret the essence of the prison problem. Researchers' conceptualization of prisonization can enhance stakeholders' understanding. For example, prisonization is a vicious cycle of terror, and inmates are simply reacting and vulnerable at attempting to survive confinement (Fabrique et al. 2007; Latessa 2004; Zingraff 1975).

Nontechnical research language demonstrates to policy makers how to create workable policies. For example, infection in the inmate population is a consequence of poor hygiene factors. Inmates sharing personal items (e.g., toothbrushes, lotion, bedding, and headphones) cause them to acquire infection requiring medical treatment. Correctional staff identifies how this regular practice spread different infections throughout the prison. Criminal-justice policy makers with understandable evidence-based research knowledge can make effective policy change (Gillespie 2005; Roberts and Hough 2005; Turabelidze et al. 2006).

Evidence-Based Research

Evidence-based research is essential to inform policy makers of research results. Research findings guide policy makers toward creating workable penal policies. In turn, the available budget for correctional facilities may increase as inmates decrease violence and ex-offenders decrease criminal activity. An example would be correctional officials measuring the outcome from inmates' drug tests and successful completion of reentry programs. This success may indicate that inmates are moving away from drugs and crime, thus creating safer communities (Jacobson 2006; Latessa 2004; Livers and Hoffman 2005; Mall 2004; Zingraff 1975).

Correctional leadership does not always agree with evidence-based research. Top leadership alone may implement policy change for the penal institutions. However, it eventually may take willingness and cooperation from correctional leaders at all levels of the penal system to implement effective policy changes. Effecting penal reform tools need cooperation from stakeholders (Jacobson 2006; Latessa 2004; Travis 2006; Winnick and Bodkin 2005).

Implementing Social Change Tools in Prison

Caution: evidence-based research alone may not convince stakeholders prison reform is necessary. Furthermore, collaborators may have different agendas essential for successful policy change. Collaborators' agendas may include the following:

1. Communities desiring more safety measures
2. Employees desiring policy change that will not affect their livelihood, job security, promotions, and safety
3. Policy makers desiring information to assist their reform agenda

Essentially, successful reform occurs with collaborators accurately interpreting research and satisfying their agendas (Jacobson 2006; Latessa 2004; Mall 2004; Turner 2006).

Once employees understand the benefits of positive change, they sense belongingness to the organization. Employees need to readjust their attitudes and beliefs toward policy change. Sequentially, for successful penal reform to occur, employees' old characteristics need changing. Additionally, correctional leaders can use staff at all grade levels to assist with implementing change. Leaders can implement positive changes that employees internalize in cultivating teamwork (Frankl 1984; Latessa 2004; Livers and Hoffman 2005; Mall 2004).

Convincing Employees

Not every organization change will satisfy employee cliques. Correctional leaders will have to convince employees that positive changes will benefit them by

a. illustrating detailed explanation why change is essential,
b. explaining how policy change will affect their job, and
c. giving mutual support to employees.

Table 2

Transformational Steps and Stages for Penal System Changes

	Transformation Stages			
Step	Employee knowledge	Employee satisfaction	Measuring change	Program evaluation
1	Vision	Personnel input	Screening	Revisit
2	Mission	Attitude	Assessment	Success
3	Positive leadership	Interpretation	Treatment	Synthesize
4	Positive thought	Professionalism	Education	Collaboration
5	Employee input	Assessment	Services	Prediction

Note: Table 2 design illustrates how successful steps and stages may transform the penal system.

Vision

A clear vision statement assists employees in identifying ultimate objectives of correctional policy. A vision statement indicates clear and precise actions essential for successful programs. It identifies certain correctional sectors needing attention. Vision statement provides correctional leaders knowledge of past successful programs and profound knowledge enhancing future programs (Latessa 2004; Mall 2004; Wheeler 1959).

A clear vision statement further assists leaders in providing employees with plain language illustrating the purpose of transformation. A vision statement demonstrates logical common sense approaches employees understand. It provides employees with simple direction and guidance while emphasizing teamwork. It eases anxiety and projects a safer, efficient working environment. Apart from the vision statement, correctional facilities also need a mission statement to be conducive toward penal change (Hatcher 2006; Livers and Hoffman 2005; Turner 2006).

Mission

Importantly, an updated correctional mission statement demonstrates how the transitional change applies to current daily prison activities. Employee cooperation comes from understanding the mission and its effect on their lives. Correctional leaders benefit from assessing employees' attitudes toward leadership (Bandura 1998; Frankl 1984; Livers and Hoffman 2005; Travis 2006).

Positive Leadership

Top leadership collaborating with upper and lower management can communicate and prepare employees for change. Correctional leaders can prepare employees by providing (a) clear instructional guideline, (b) two-way communication, (c) advance training, and (d) proper resources. Leadership implementing a central training support system will improve employees' self-efficacy, positive thought, and improve inmate treatment (Bandura 1998; Hatcher 2006; Livers and Hoffman 2005; Thomas et al. 1978).

Effective Training

Effective training focuses on getting employees thinking positively about their work environment and inmate safety. Effective training allows employees to contribute in rehabilitating offenders as respectful law-abiding citizens. The benefits of this incredible training contribute to correctional institutions and transform inmates'/employees' relationship (Jacobson 2006; Latessa 2004; Winnick and Bodkin 2005).

Transforming successful inmates'/employees' relationships requires effective training. Successful workable programs come with proper training and articulated guidance. Proper training satisfies employees and allows them to improve prison programs. (Livers and Hoffman 2005; Wheeler 1959; Winnick and Bodkin 2005; Zingraff 1975)

Personnel Satisfaction

Satisfied employees come from leaders who provide (a) a secure work environment, (b) positive feedback, (c) additional training, (d) emphasis on ethical behavior, and (e) positive encouragement. Assessing employee satisfaction promotes effective growth and development (Hatcher 2006; Johnson and Dobrzanska 2005; Livers and Hoffman 2005; Perry 2001).

Assessment

Assessing employee readiness toward change, leaders can implement effective policy. Assessment measures employee readiness, barriers to communication, and strengths. Proper assessment prepares employees for policy change and measures their level of acceptance (Chlup 2006; Kenemore and Roldan 2006; Latessa 2004; Roberts and Hough 2005).

Accepting Change

Employees who accept policy change give leaders added confidence to implement more programs. Accepting policy change assures leaders employees will perform their duties. Hiring a new supervisor, either downsizing, or promoting employees give leaders positive attitudes. Accepting external policy changes provide correctional personnel with a trouble-free environment (Alvin 2005; Latessa 2004; Livers and Hoffman 2005; Wodahl 2006).

Employee acceptance of change provides leaders ways to measure policy change. However, implementing programs change include researchers measuring the effect policy change has on inmates' motivation. Researchers can measure at least four previous successful and unsuccessful programs (Johnson and Dobrzanska 2005; Kenemore and Roldan 2006; Livers and Hoffman 2005).

Measuring Changes

Researchers can measure the external effect policy change has on inmates internal motivation. Another approach focusing on policy change is "RESTART—Reentry and Enforcement Services Targeting Addictions, Rehabilitation and Treatment" (Akbar 2004; Bandura 1973; Livers and Hoffman 2005; Reuss 2003).

Researchers can provide leaders with results from measuring the effect policy change has on penal programs. Leaders take the research findings and use it for implementing future programs. Evaluating inmate motivation can become a regular part of correctional institutions. Outcome measure provides an excellent base knowledge guideline for leaders to continue implementing suitable programs (Livers and Hoffman 2005; Mall 2004; Travis 2006). Outcome measures benefit correctional institutions by (a) screening inmates; (b) assessing inmates; (c) designing inmate treatment, education/vocation, and transitional services; (d) evaluating outcome measures. They enhance future policy change by explaining shortcomings in correctional institutions and evaluating change.

Evaluation-outcome measures enable leaders to revisit past programs and services that have had an impact on inmates' success. They can review successful programs by improving on them while avoiding unsuccessful ones. Leaders can have an impact on inmates' rehabilitation and liberate them with proper delivery of service (Alvin 2005; Buell 2005; Latessa 2004).

Delivery of Services

Delivery of services and resources increases inmate cooperation, decrease violence, and reduce prisonization. Leaders acquiring the right resources for employees enable them to adjust better to future changes. Lastly, proper delivery of services ensures public safety, employee satisfaction, and inmates' successful rehabilitation (Johnson and Dobrzanska 2005; Latessa 2004; Livers and Hoffman 2005).

Proper delivery of services enhances correctional institutions. Proper resources reduce inmate dysfunction and dependency. This guide attempts to cover the many solutions that reduce prisonization. It synthesizes essential theoretical and current aspects of inmate human development. Fortunately, there remains a fundamental demand for further research. Below is an additional reference list for further reading about effective solutions in reducing prisonization (DeLisi 2003; Gillespie 2003; Lehrer 2001; Wheeler 1959).

Closing Statement

Controlling the gradual effects of prisonization requires assertiveness from all stakeholders. Criminal-justice policy makers can study sufficient causes of prisonization implementing workable policies combating prisonization. Correctional institutions combating prisonization focus on inmate needs and employee satisfaction. Allowing family participation gives inmates hope for a better life after prison. Implementing effective training give employees a sense of pride, professionalism, and job security. Inmates can combat prisonization by developing self-control, self-motivation, and choosing adjusting strategies that allow independent actions.

Although some problems occur because of importation, this guide primarily suggests that prisonization emerges from socialization through violence, intimidation, and length of sentence. Researchers explaining prison socialization can present it in a clear and understandable language providing stakeholders accurate information that properly measure and evaluate change. Proper communication of the facts will ensure stakeholders collaboration toward controlling the gradual effect of prisonization.

Additional Reading List

References

Bornus, D. 2007. "The Correctional Tetrahedron: An Effective Correctional Management Model." Corrections Today 69 (30): 64-66.

Buell, M. 2005. "Women in Contact with the Criminal Justice System Have Specific Needs." Corrections Today 67 (7): 28-30.

Clarke, H., and M. Layman. 2004. "Recruitment: Tools, Tips and Practical Application." Corrections Today 66 (5): 80, 82-85.

Duff, P. 1998. "Crime Control, Due Process and 'The Case for the Prosecution': A Problem of Terminology?" The British Journal of Criminology 38 (4): 611-615.

Evans, D. 2007. "Sharing Knowledge on Effective Community Supervision Programs." Corrections Today 69 (2): 108-109.

Fry, R. 2002. "Positive Regard." Community Corrections Report on Law and Corrections Practice 9 (5): 71.

Gomez, J. 2007. "Correctional Coaching: Teaching Managers to be Coaches." Corrections Today 69 (1): 43-45.

Hickman, R. 2007. "Politics, Power, the Press and Prisons." Corrections Today 69 (1): 46-48.

Livers, M., and N. Hoffman. 2005. "A Renewed Focus on Mission and Vision: Maryland's Strategy for Creating Cultural Change." Corrections Today 67 (7): 56-62.

Livers, M., and T. Hiers. 2007. "Gender-Responsive Programs: Addressing the Needs of Female Offenders." Corrections Today 69 (4): 26-29.

McCourt, M. 2005. "The Day Change Is Good. Unless It's Happening to You." Security 42 (12): 7.

McElhaney, J. 2005. "The Real Message." ABA Journal 79: 74.

Moffat, K. 2006. "Pandora's Box: Risk/Need and Gender-Responsive." Corrections Today 5 (1): 183.

Moses, M., and E. Kirschbaum. 2007. "From Needles and Thread to Legislative Mandates: New Hampshire Addresses the Needs of Women in Custody." Corrections Today 69 (4): 48-51.

Moss, A. 2007. "The Prison Rape Elimination Act: Implications for Women and Girls." Corrections Today 69 (4): 44-47, 70.

Potter, R. 2007. "For Good Intentions to Evidence-Based: Paving the Right Road." Corrections Today 69 (3): 74-75.

Riley, J. 2000. "Sensemaking in Prison: Inmate Identity as a Working Understanding." Highland Heights 17 (2): 359.

Travis, M. 2007. "One Hundred to One: Odds Are That Female Inmates Are Not So Bad After All." Corrections Today 69 (4): 72-74.

White, T. 2006. "Process and Outcome Measurement: Cornerstone of Achilles' Heel of Evidence-Based Practice?" Community Corrections Report on Law and Corrections Practice 13 (5): 65.

Whiteacre, K. 2006. "Measuring Job Satisfaction and Stress at a Community Corrections Center: An Evidence-Based Study." Corrections Today 68(3): 70-73.

Wilkinson, R., E. Rhine, and M. Hurley. 2005. "Reentry in Ohio Corrections: A Catalyst for Change." Journal of Correctional Education 56 (2): 158.

Conclusion

The dark days of mass incarceration may be obsolete once people acquire accurate knowledge about prison conditions. Knowledge in its correct context may enhance policies, rules, and regulations. This knowledge base extends out to individuals who happened to find themselves confined in prison. Prisons do not necessary have to represent inhumane treatment, inmate violence, and prisonization.

Implementing the right changes in the penal system may result in successful programs. Programs that send formal inmates back home as law-abiding citizens exemplify right changes. First, correctional officials need to explain the change through the organization vision statement. A vision statement that is clear and understandable may allow employees to work as a team. Along with the vision statement (i.e., how, why, when, what, and where) is the mission statement.

The precise mission statement of the organization includes and explains the procedures of daily duties and the requirements expected from employees. For example, female inmates have special needs, and the prison mission statement may include a listing of their fundamental needs so employees understand those needs. Male inmates have special needs different from females; employees need to understand what those needs are. The mission statement requires employees' participation for successful outcome.

Employees may need additional training to adherence to the mission and policy changes. The employees' training, vision, and mission statement will benefit the employees as well as the inmates. Knowing that the change will benefit interest parties may reflect a favorable attitude from stakeholders for more changes in the future.

Policy makers' decision depends on the public perception of prisons. When the public perceive a need to continue rehabilitation, consequently policy makers may have to follow their wishes. The public may view prison as an aggressive institution, or they may view it as being too aggressive and need to change. Whatever the fundamental demand becomes, policy makers need some guidance to make hard decisions.

Researchers are the essential guidance policy makers depend on. Researchers investigate the significant problems and report findings that may improve the penal system. However, researchers have a responsibility to conduct ethical and reliable studies that shows a clear relationship between variables. In addition, it is essential that researchers use simple nontechnical language so stakeholders can interpret the right meaning from the findings. Lastly, success comes with collaboration, clear communication, and a willingness to change.

References

Akbar, N. 1995. Natural Psychology and Human Transformation. Tallahassee, Florida: Mind Production & Associates, Inc.

Akbar, N. 2004. The Community of Self. Tallahassee, Florida: Mind Production & Associates, Inc.

Akbar, N. 1993. Visions for Black men. Tallahassee: Mind Productions & Associates, Inc.

Alvin, B. 2005. "Incarceration as a Failed Policy." Corrections Today 67 (5): 1-3.

Bandura, A. 1973. Aggression: A Social Learning Analysis. New Jersey: Prentice Hall.

Bandura, A., and R. Walters. 1963. Social Learning and Personality Development. New York: Holt, Rinehart and Winston, Inc.

Bandura, A. 1998. Self-Efficacy: The Exercise of Control. New York: W.H. Freeman and Company.

Buell, M. 2005. "Women in Contact with the Criminal Justice System Have Specific Needs." Corrections Today 67 (7): 28-29.

Chlup, D. 2006. "The Legacy of Miriam Van Waters: The Warden Who Would Be the Teacher First. Journal of Correctional Education 57 (2): 158-187.

Craig, E. 2006. "Building Bonds from the Inside Out." Corrections Today 68 (7): 42-45.

Currie, E. 1993. "Shifting the Balance on Social Action and the Future of Criminological Research." Journal of Research in Crime and Delinquency 30 (4): 478-484.

DeLisi, M. 2003. "Criminal Careers behind Bars." Behavioral Science and the Law 21: 653-669. Retrieved from *www.interscience.wiley.com*.

Fabrique, N., S. Romano, G. Vecchi, and V. Hasselt. 2007. "Understanding Stockholm Syndrome." FBI Law Enforcement Bulletin 76 (7): 10-15.

Frankl, V. 1984. Man's Search for Meaning. New York: Washington Square Press.

Frankl, V. 2000. Man's Search for Ultimate Meaning. New York: Basic Books.

Gillespie, W. 2003. Prisonization: Individual and Institutional Factors Affecting Inmate Conduct. LFB Scholarly Publishing. 177.

Gillespie, W. 2005. "Racial Differences in Violence and Self-Esteem among Prison Inmates." American Journal of Criminal Justice 29 (2): 161-185.

Grounds, A. 2002. "Prisons and Prisoners." Criminal Behaviour and Mental Health 12: S24-S34.

Haney, C. 2001. "The Psychological Impact of Incarceration: Implication for Post-Prison Adjustment." University of California. 1-17.

Hatcher, L. 2006. "Security Threat Groups: It Is More Than Managing Gangs in a Local Facility." Corrections Today 68 (2): 54-58.

Jacobson, M. 2006. "Reversing the Punitive Turn: The Limits and Promise of Current Research." Criminoloy & Public Policy 5 (2): 277-284.

Jensen, G., and D. Jones. 2001. "Perspectives on Inmates Culture: A Study of Women in Prison." National Science Foundation: 590-603.

Johnson, R., and A. Dobrzanska. 2005. "Mature Coping among Life-Sentenced Inmates: An Exploratory Study of Adjustment." Corrections Compendium 30 (6): 8-12.

Kenemore, T and I. Roldan. 2006. "Staying Straight: Lessons from Ex-offenders." Clinical Social Work Journal 34 (1): 5-21.

Kerley, K., T. Matthews, and T. Blanchard. 2005. "Religiosity, Religious Participation, and Negative Prison Behaviors." Journal for the Scientific of Religion 44 (4): 443-457.

Latessa, E. 2004. "The Challenge of Change: Correctional Programs and Evidence-Based Practices." Criminology & Public Policy 3 (4): 547-560.

Leder, D. 2004. "Imprisoned Bodies: The Life-World of the Incarcerated." Social Justice 31 (1-2): 51-66.

Lehrer, E. 2001. "Hell behind Bars. The Crime That Dare Not Speak Its Name." National Review: 24-26.

Livers, M., and N. Hoffman. 2005. "A Renewed Focus on Mission and Vision: Maryland's Strategy for Creating Culture Change." Corrections Today 67 (7): 56-62.

Mall, M. 2004. "Outcome Measures: An Excellent Management Tool in Corrections." Corrections Today 66 (7): 24.

Merton, R. 1968. Social Theory and Social Structure. New York: The Free Press.

O'Connor, P. 2001. "The Prison Cage as Home for African American Men." Journal of African American Men 6 (1): 71-86.

Perry, M. 2001. "The Games Inmates Play." Corrections Today 63 (2): 2-4.

Drislane, R., and G. Parkinson. Online dictionary of the social sciences. Athabasca University ICAAP: Canada's Open University. *http://bitbuckel.icaap.org*. Retrieved 10/10/2007.

Reuss, A. 2003. "Taking a Long Hard Look at Imprisonment." The Howard Journal 42 (5): 426-436.

Roberts, J., and M. Hough. 2005. "The State of the Prisons: Exploring Public Knowledge and Opinion." The Howard Journal 44 (3): 286-306.

Rodriguez, D. 2003. "State Terror and the Reproduction of Imprisoned Dissent." Social Identities 9 (2): 183-203.

Stevens, D. 1998. "The Impact of Time-Served and Regime on Prisoners' Anticipation of Crime: Female Prisonisation Effects." The Howard Journal 37 (2): 188-205.

Thomas, C., D. Petersen, and R. Zingraff. 1978. "Structural and Social Psychological Correlates of Prisonization." Criminology 16 (3): 384-393.

Torres, Sam. 2006. "Behind Bars in America." Federal Probation 70 (3): 63.

Travis, M. 2006. "Leading the Change in Facility Transition." Corrections Today 68 (5): 54-58.

Turabelidze, G., M. Lin, B. Wolkoff, D. Dodson, S. Gladbach, and B. Zhu. 2006. "Personal Hygiene and Methicillin-Resistant Staphylococcus aureus infection." Emerging Infectious Diseases 12 (3): 422-427.

Turner, J. 2006. "Tyranny, Freedom and Social Structure: Escaping our Theoretical Prisons." The British Journal of Social Psychology 45: 41-46.

US Department of Justice, Bureau of Justice Statistics. 2005. Sourcebook of Criminal Justice Statistic Online. *www.albany.edu/sourcebook/pdt/t6332005.pdf.*

Valle, A., V. Huang, and M. Spira. 2006. "The Prison Industrial Complex." International Feminist Journal of Politics: 130-144.

Wheeler, S. 1959. "Socialization in Correctional Communities." American Sociological Review: 697-712.

Winnick, T., and M. Bodkin. 2005. "Inmates' Perception of Stigma and Anticipated Coping Orientations Upon Release."

Paper presented at the annual meeting of the American Sociological Association, Philadelphia, August 12.

Wodahl, E. 2006. "The Challenges of Prisoner Reentry from a Rural Perspective." Western Criminology Review 7 (2): 23-47.

Zingraff, M. 1975. "Prisonization as an Inhibitor of Effective Resocialization." Criminology 13 (3): 367-388.

www.ingramcontent.com/pod-product-compliance
Lightning Source LLC
Chambersburg PA
CBHW061220280526
45784CB00006B/2566